DEFYING EXPECTATIONS

A housewife guide to financial empowerment

Wealthy Path: Empowering Housewives
via Financial Wisdom on Their Journey.

RENU SINGHAL GUPTA

BlueRose ONE
Stories Matter
New Delhi • London

BLUEROSE PUBLISHERS
India | U.K.

For permissions requests or inquiries regarding this publication, please contact:

BLUEROSE PUBLISHERS
www.BlueRoseONE.com
info@bluerosepublishers.com
+91 8882 898 898
+4407342408967

ISBN: 978-93-5819-674-0

Cover Design: Muskan Sachdeva
Typesetting: Pooja Sharma

First Edition: March 2024

I take this opportunity to thank all those who believed in me and also those who did not. As the former truly encouraged me with their positivity while The latter brought in me the spirit to prove them wrong and egged me on.

I was a housewife, though a qualified ICWA, I could not do much about my qualification because of my husband's transferable job and my two kids. I Chose to be a housewife and also suffered frequent criticism because of it but that did not deter me from taking whole hearted care of my kids and my house. because neglecting my kids was not an option for me. It was my choice to make and I made it with pride. Today when I see my children doing well I feel pride, joy and satisfaction that nothing else can give.

But the desire to do something of my own was also there deep down within me and I had the confidence that I could do it. It was then that I enrolled myself in an NSE certified short term course in share market.

When I took the step to resume my studies i. e to do a professional course related to share market, I also started with a lot of misgiving and self doubt which being human we all do from time to time.

It took a lot of courage to step out of my comfort zone with 2 grown up kids and a well to do household. I took a metro daily and walked a good 1 km to reach my classes. It was quiet tiring at times since I used to finish housework before going to these afternoon classes. soon I got used to the daily regimen of taking classes, studying and taking exams. My hard work paid off and I passed the course in flying colors.

These classes gave me the confidence to dabble in stock market. After completing the course I dint immediately started investing. I studied the market for sometime and did my own research on the stocks that I wanted to invest and then entered the market with as little as rs 25000/. We have been taught in our course that one should invest the amount that one can afford to lose. Initially I did incur some losses but I learned a lot from my experience.

I opened 2-3 SIP in some good mutual funds and when there were sufficient amount like rs 20, 000 or more, I withdrew that and invested in shares. After sometime I started making profits which gave lot of confidence to me. I re invested any profit that I made and also any lumpsum that was gifted to me. After 7 to 8 years of being in the stock market I have a modest investment of around 10 lakhs now. I feel excited to share my investment journey so that other women are inspired to do so. by just investing 4k to 5k per month I was able to achieve it. We women are great savers but most of us don't know how to invest. Financial knowledge leads to financial empowerment. My simple steps to achieve this goal will be illustrated in this book in coming chapters.

Even a housewife can become investors. How would you like to plan a vacation or contribute in studies of your child or just go for a simple shopping trip for yourself. Some simple investment tools can empower you to do just that. Never underestimate yourself. The hand that rocks the cradle rules the world. This saying will come true once you financially empower yourself.

After doing the NSE certified course in shares I also attended lots of workshops in which I gained lot of technical knowledge in graphs, charts, ratio analysis. All these are good but one has to actually start investing to actually learn how the market works. Through my own experience in the market I have come up with some simple and workable steps to how to invest in the market and make profits as well.

Some of these are as follows-

1. TO invest in share market the first thing needed is to open a D Mat account. It could be in a bank or an independent broker.

2. Download an App which gives details of shares and ups and downs in the market on a daily basis like -Money control and Stock edge.

3. Keep a daily check on NIFTY and SENSEX

4. Do your own research of the stocks before investing, research includes-

    1. keeping a track of some stocks daily like their high and low of the day, one can also get details like 52 week high and low and also monthly, daily and yearly charts of the stocks.

    2. The story of the company. -like what is the history of the company, their products, growth, deals made etc.

    3. latest news of the company in newspapers, magazines etc.

    4. The stocks which are on your radar should be of good quality companies, so that even if the market goes down, they make money in the long term.

Some people say, 'oh it is so simple to make money in the market, buy the shares when they are going down and sell when they go up', . but it is not so simple as I found through my experience. When there is downward trend i. e it is a bear market, we don't know how far it will fall and when it is a Bull trend i. e market is rising we don't know how far it will rise. So to time the market as to when to enter is very crucial and really important.

.

Contents

WHY SHOULD WE INVEST

Investing is a crucial aspect of financial empowerment, and it holds several benefits that everyone should consider. Here are some reasons why investing is important:

1. Wealth Creation: Investing allows individuals to grow their wealth over time. By putting money into various investment vehicles such as stocks, mutual funds, or real estate, one has the potential to earn higher returns compared to keeping money idle in a savings account. Over the long term, investing can significantly increase one's net worth and provide financial security.
2. Beating Inflation: Inflation erodes the purchasing power of money over time. The prices of goods and services tend to increase, meaning that the same amount of money will buy fewer items in the future, or purchasing something today will cost much more after a few years. Investing helps combat inflation by generating returns that outpace the rate of inflation. This way, investors can preserve and increase the value of their money.

3. Financial Goals: Investing plays a crucial role in achieving long-term financial goals. Whether it's saving for retirement, funding a child's education, buying a house, or planning a vacation, investing can provide the necessary returns to fulfill these objectives. By starting early and being consistent with investments, individuals have a better chance of meeting their financial aspirations.
4. Passive Income: Some investments, such as dividend-paying stocks, rental properties, or bonds, can generate regular income in the form of dividends, rent, or interest payments. This passive income can supplement one's primary source of income and provide financial stability. Passive income can also be reinvested, accelerating wealth accumulation.
5. Diversification and Risk Management: Investing in a diversified portfolio spread across different asset classes helps manage risk. Diversification involves investing in various industries, sectors, and geographic regions to reduce the impact of potential losses. By spreading investments, one can minimize the risk associated with any single investment and protect their capital.
6. Retirement Planning: Investing is essential for retirement planning. By starting early and consistently contributing to retirement accounts

like 401(k)s or IRAs, individuals can build a substantial nest egg for their retirement years. The power of compounding, where investment returns generate additional returns over time, is advantageous when investing for the long term.

7. Financial Independence: Successful investing can provide financial independence and freedom. It allows individuals to rely less on paycheck-to-paycheck living and creates opportunities for personal and professional growth. Financial independence means having the means to pursue one's passions, take calculated risks, and enjoy a comfortable lifestyle without financial constraints.
8. Knowledge and Personal Growth: Investing requires continuous learning and staying updated with market trends and economic factors. Engaging in investment activities broadens one's knowledge about businesses, industries, and the global economy. It can also improve analytical skills, decision-making abilities, and financial literacy, leading to personal growth and empowerment.

Investing is not without risks, and individuals should carefully evaluate their risk tolerance, financial goals, and seek professional advice if needed. However, with proper knowledge, research, and a long-term perspective, investing can be a rewarding endeavor that contributes to overall financial well-being.

Only actors or lottery winners can get rich overnight. The rest of us have to take small concrete steps to build wealth. So one should not fall into the trap of easy money and ponzi schemes.

One should save aggressively and invest regularly to achieve one's financial goals. Various tools of investment will be discussed in the next chapter.

TYPES / OPTIONS OF INVESTMENT

In the world of investment, there are various types of financial instruments and options available to investors. Choosing the best investment options is important for all income groups. There are several long term and short term investment options that can cater to different risk appetites, and financial objectives. Here are some common types/options in investment:

Listed below are some of the best investment options in India:

1. Fixed Deposits[FD]

   Fixed deposits are considered the safest, stable among the best short term investment options. One can invest in fixed deposits for the following reasons:

   1. To accumulate good returns from various FD schemes, especially when FD rates are increasing.
   2. Hassle free renewal each year will give compounding returns
   3. Fund remains safe

4. The Principal amount will not diminish.
5. No market fluctuation effect
6. Guaranteed returns

All these reasons make a fixed deposit deposit one of the best investment options, which also offers guaranteed returns. If one is seeking a healthy balance between returns and safety then one should start investing as soon as possible

2. Stocks : Investments are often seen synonymous with stocks. Stocks represent ownership in a company. When you buy shares of a company's stock, you become a partial owner of that company. As the company's value increases, the value of your shares also rises, allowing you to potentially earn profits through capital appreciation and dividends. By buying a company's share, one also get the right to be involved in company meetings and have your say on company's decisions. Also, you get profits as distribution in proportion to one's shareholding in the company.

3. Mutual funds: While investment in mutual funds is subjected to market risk, one has to evaluate risk before investing. If one understands the market and its risks then mutual fund can become one's best investment option to grow and multiply money. You can

create an investment portfolio based on your risk preferences.

If you have a lower risk appetite and want a fixed income from mutual funds, monthly systematic investment plans or systematic withdrawal plans can be good investment options.

4. Bonds: Just like individuals, companies and government bodies need funds for infrastructural development and social programs, for which they issue bond to the pubic markets. When you buy a bond, you are effectively lending money to the issuer for a specified period. In return, the issuer pays you periodic interest payments and repays the principal amount at maturity.

   In other words, bonds are fixed income investment options that cover the loan made by an investor to a corporate or governmental borrower.

   What makes them one of the best investment plan in india is that the terms of fixed interest payment, loan principal, and tenure are all included in the bond details. Hence, it assures you of the safety of your investment along with an additional return.

5. Post Office Saving Schemes: These are deposit avenues for investors made available by India Post, the body that controls the postal chain in India. This investment option was once introduced to help people inculcate the habit os disciplined savings in life while also providing investment avenues to aid in financial planning.

   What makes these schemes good investment option is the ease of enrolment or application You can invest in these saving schemes by visiting nearest ost office branch.

   Saving schemes that fall under post office investments include:

   *Post Office Savings Account

   *Post Office Time Deposit Account(TD)

   *5-year Recurring Deposit Account (RD)

   * Monthly Income Scheme Account (MIS), and many others

   *Senior Citizen Saving Scheme(SCSS)

6. ULIP. Another investment option for individuals who want market linked returns along with insurance is Unit Linked Insurance Plan (ULIP). You can buy a life insurance which helps to invest in different funds and give you a life cover option at the same time. ULIP has

become one of the best investment plans in India.

This top investment option in India offers dual benefits of insurance and market investments, which helps you systematically grow your money. You can choose the most suitable policy tenure based on whether you prefer long term or short term investment options. Additionally ULIP also offers tax benefits under section 80 C of the income tax act 1961. Some of the plans in India are:-

1. LIC Endowment plus
2. TATA AIA LIFE Unit linked plans
3. ICICI Pru Signature

7. Exchange-Traded Funds (ETFs): ETFs are similar to mutual funds in that they also hold a diversified portfolio of securities. However, they are traded on stock exchanges like individual stocks, allowing investors to buy and sell them throughout the trading day at market prices.

8. National Pension Scheme(NPS):National Pension Scheme is a government initiated investment option, which have the objective of securing the financial life of a citizen after retirement. NPS is the best investment option if you have minimal or no risk appetite and want to save for your retirement.

Under this scheme, you can save in government bonds, equity, and other alternative investment options as per your preference. Not only NPS is one of the best investment options, but it is also safest option to save and grow money for retirement. You can start investing in National Pension Scheme starting from rs 500, having interest rate of 8 - 10%

9. Public Provident Fund(PPF) : PPF is a government supported savings scheme. It is open to everyone employed, unemployed, self-employed or retired. It has a minimum lock in period of 15 years. It is an excellent investment option for people uncomfortable in taking risks. While the returns may not be very high as interest rate is fixed (current PPF rate is 7. 1%p. a, that is compounded annually) it offers safe investment with lot of tax benefit. PPF Interest and maturity amount are tax free under section 80C of the Income tax Act, 1961.

10. Options: Options are financial derivatives that provide the buyer with the right, but not the obligation, to buy (call option) or sell (put option) an underlying asset at a specified price (strike price) on or before a predetermined date (expiration date). Options can be used for speculation, hedging, or generating income.
11. Commodities: Commodities are physical goods such as gold, oil, agricultural products, etc. Investors can buy commodities directly or invest in commodity futures contracts to speculate on the price movements of these assets.
12. Forex (Foreign Exchange): Forex trading involves buying and selling currencies in the foreign exchange market. Investors can profit from changes in currency exchange rates.
13. Cryptocurrencies: Cryptocurrencies are digital or virtual currencies that use cryptography for security. Popular examples include Bitcoin, Ethereum, and Ripple. Investing in cryptocurrencies carries significant risk due to their high volatility.

Each type of investment has its own risk profile and potential for returns, and it's essential for investors to conduct thorough research and consider their financial goals before making investment decisions.

Diversification is often recommended to spread risk across different assets and improve the chances of achieving long-term financial objectives.

HOW TO PICK GOOD QUALITY STOCKS

1. Pick the stocks of the companies that have great growth stories. Which have given consistent good returns in past 5-10 years. Examples being Reliance, Tata group shares, L&T and so on

   Let us see the growth story of Reliance Industries-

   According to the data from Investing. Com India, the Share price of Reliance Industries ltd(RELI) has increased by 153. 21% in the last 5 years.

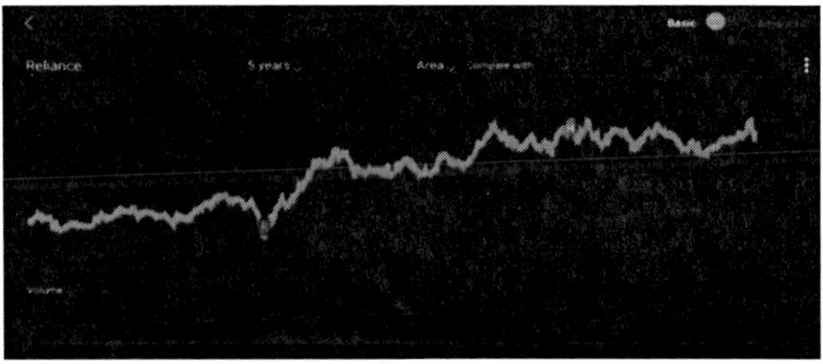

As we can see from the graph the share price of reliance in march 2019 was around rs 1000/ and in 2020 when the whole world was reeling with the shock of outbreak of covid it went as low as aroundrs800/. It again bounced back and

continued its upward journey. As of now its share price on 4th august 2023 is rs 2509. 55/.

Its growth story is the growth story of INDIA. Its operations range from exploration and production of oil and gas to the manufacture of petroleum products, polyester products, polyester intermediaries, plastics, polymer intermediaries, chemicals, synthetic textiles and fabrics.

Reliance Industries share price in the year 1990 was rs 11. 74. If you had invested Rs 10, 000/ in Reliance Industries in 1990, in 33 years, your investment would have grown to rs 21. 94 lakhs by the end of 2023. This represents a positive return of 21836. 9% from 1990 to 2023, with a compound annual growth rate (CAGR)OF 17. 7%.

As seen from the Reliance share journey, the returns have been spectacular.

Likewise we can do some other case studies too.

Let's do the case study of Tata Motors.

It is a major part of $100 billion Tata Group. It was founded in 1945 as TELCO (Tata Engineering and Locomotive Co. Ltd. to manufacture commercial vehicles. The major products that the company deals in include trucks, passenger cars, vans, buses, coaches, military vehicles and construction equipments. As of now it is the 17 th biggest motor vehicle production company in the world, 4th biggest truck producer and 2nd biggest bus manufacturer.

GRAPH OF TATA MOTORS(Last 5 years)

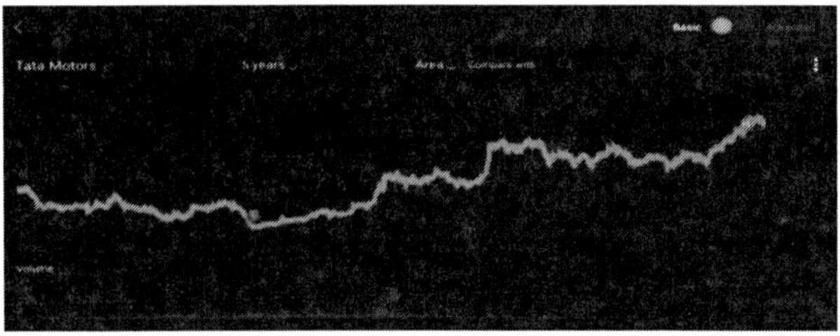

As seen from the graph the share price of Tata Motors have grown from around rs 200/ in year 2019 to rs 618/ in august 2023. That comes out to be a growth of over 200% thereby growing investors wealth also by the same percentage.

If we see the performance of the stock in last 20 years, it has given blockbuster returns to the shareholders. If an investor had put in rs 10, 000/ in this tata group stock in august 2003, it would have swelled to around rs 1, 34 lack according to the calculations.

As we can see from both these case studies that both RELIANCE andTATA MOTORS have been leaders in their categories, They have earned their name and reputation over the years by consistent performance and growth. They can always be added to the portfolio knowing that they will give good returns.

Their have been many other industries that have given spectacular growth and results in India like L&T, ITC, TATA Steel, Tech Mahindra and so on. We need to study the company and look at its performance before purchasing its stocks. These companies about which we have discussed are generally more expensive than the small caps, so one needs to time the entry level of these. But their consistent good returns make them very good long term investment.

2. Next we can also pick stocks which are cyclic in nature. Which means that when the industry to which they belong is in boom, they will also rise.

   Key takeaways of Cyclic Stocks are_

   *Cyclic stocks are affected by macroeconomic changes, where its returns follow the cycles of an economy.

   * Cyclic stocks are more volatile than non cyclic or defensive stocks. Defensive stocks include stocks of consumer goods and services that people continue to buy through all kinds of business cycles

*Cyclic stocks usually have higher volatility and are expected to produce higher returns during periods of economic strength.

Sectors which are cyclic in nature include

a, Auto

b. Pharma

c. Metals

d. Media

c. Reality

d. Travel

Companies related to these sectors like car manufacturer, Airlines. property developers, hotels and restaurants etc. When the economy is doing well, people can afford to buy new cars, upgrade their homes, shop and travel. If the economy is doing well and government is also spending on infrastructure projects then need for metals, cement and all also increases making them a good investment option.

When the economy is doing poorly and recession is severe, cyclic stocks can become worthless and companies may go out of business. Investors should be careful about their positions in cyclic stocks but should not avoid them altogether. Their is some predictability in their movement so investors should time the market to enter these stocks. Although they are volatile however they offer great potential for growth because they tend to outperform the the market during period of economic growth.

These stocks can be good long term options because then their volatility is managed.

Let us take up a case Analysis of Tata Steel

TATA STEEL

Tata Iron and Steel Company(TISCO)

Tata Iron and Steel(TISCO) was founded by Jamsetji Nusserwanji Tata and established by Sir Dorabji Tata on26 August 1907. TISCO. TISCO started pig iron production in 1911 and began producing steel in 1912 as a branch of Jamshetji's Tata Group. The first steel ingot was manufactured on 16 February 1912.

Tata Steel has become one of the leading steel manufacturers across the globe in last 116 years. The Company Is hopeful of lasting another 100 years on the back of its multi-generational employees and people centric work culture. With clear focus and targets in sight, T. V Narendran, CEO AND MD of Tata Steel, explains how a large part of future growth will take place in India due to the infra push of the government and its investment in future and sustainable technology.

The below image has the year end share price of Tata Steel from year 1994 to 2021, 27 years of data.

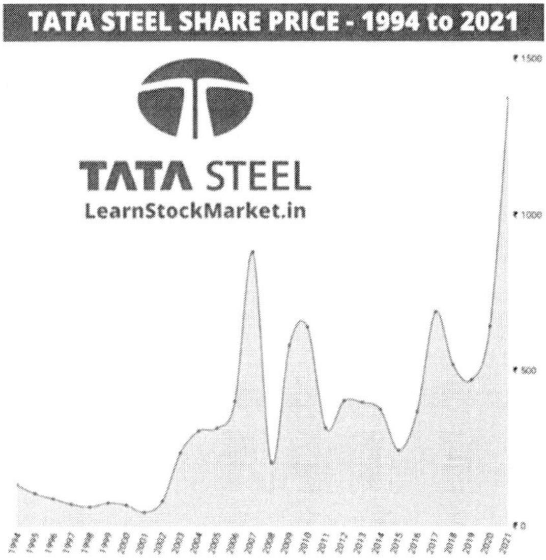

As seen from the above graph Tata Steel prices remained constant for a long time, without much action and rose to all time high in year 2006 only to fall again in year 2008 and all gains erased. Then again didn't rise much and rose from end of year 2018 and continued to rise to an all time high in august 2021, It reached its 52 week high of 1, 534. 60/ on august 16th, 2021.

In the last 25 years if the Tata Steel has doubled investor's wealth within a single year, 2003, 2007, 2009 and 2021.

At the same time. crashes have been quiet frequent too. Four years out of the last 25, stock has crashed more than 30%. In 2008, Tata steel lost 80%of its value

Two important points to be noted here are

1. When you buy a company which has short, but strong cycles like Tata Steel-you have to get the entry and exit right. Metal sector has shorter cycles. That is the reason stock in the metal sector are bought when the PE (Price to earning)is high and sold when the PE is low.

2 One should not allocate a large percentage of one's portfolio in such cyclic stocks because of the risk involved. It is always better not to allocate more than 5 %to such stocks and a maximum of 20% to one sector -even if you are extremely bullish on the sector. This is because the performance (or non performance) depends on various global factors which are beyond your control.

However, even though Tata Steel has been through several ups and down cycles-those who have stayed invested for decades -have made decent returns. as long as they did not pick the worse time to buy shares of the company.

I bought Tata Steel in 2017 at around rs600/, for some time it remained constant and then started to fall in 2018 and 2019, I kept holding on to it as I knew that it is a good company and believed in its potential, till in 2020- 2021 it started rising and my patience had paid off, I sold some part in 2021 and held on to some shares. My patience again paid off as recently in 2023 there was a stock split of 1:10 and number of my shares grew 10 fold but though the value remained the same, I'm hoping that the value will continue to rise as government's push towards infrastructure of the country is rising.

Long -Term investing is difficult, it is easy to hold a company when it is rising, it is easy to hold a company which is already in loss. But it is very difficult to see big gains vanish after which you decide to stay invested.

If you lose your patience and exit here, you would have ended up selling Tata Steel at a time when it was about to rise more than 3 times in one of the fastest bull markets the Indian stock markets has seen.

If you bought in 2011 and held till 2021 _it would have been a ride full of difficulties, but the returns of the 2021 ensured Tata Steel outperformed FD massively.

If you can avoid buying when everyone is buying the same stock and avoid selling when everyone is selling -there is no reason why you cant make money even in Cyclic companies like Tata Steel.

3. Keeping updated with information : Another way of finding good stocks could be from reading information on the upcoming industries in the Magazines, Newspapers and Internet. One can identify new growth sectors while going through the information. Like India is regarded as the growth story all over the world, the reason being its potential and development projects like infrastructure development being taken by our government. So the upcoming sector is Infrastructure and other related industries with it like Cement industry.

   India is the second largest producer of cement in the world. China is the largest producer of cement in the world.

   In FY 2022, domestic production of cement stood at 356 million tons, up from 296 million tons in FY 2021. In terms of volume, cement consumption reached 355. 46 million tons in FY 2022 and is expected to reach 450. 78 million tons by 2027.

Let us study ULTRA TECH CEMENT

The most prosperous Cement company in India, the third most successful Cement company worldwide, apart from China, and the most prosperous Cement manufacturer worldwide are all UltraTech Cement. In addition, UltraTech Cement is the biggest cement producer in India.

India Cement Industry Market Share 2022 (Listed Companies) PIE CHART

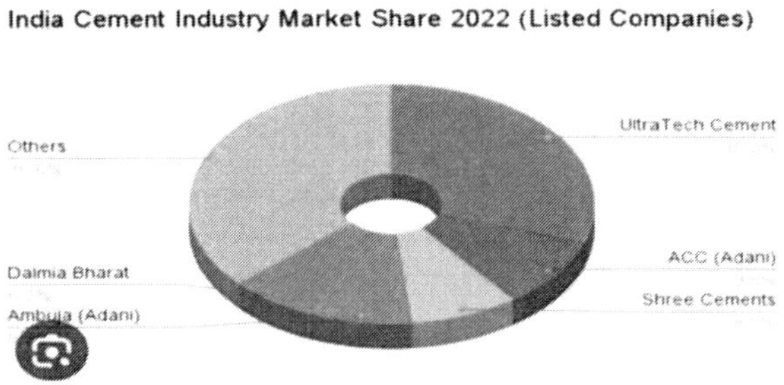

GRAPH OF SHARE PRICE OF ULTRATECH CEMENT IN LAST 5 YEARS

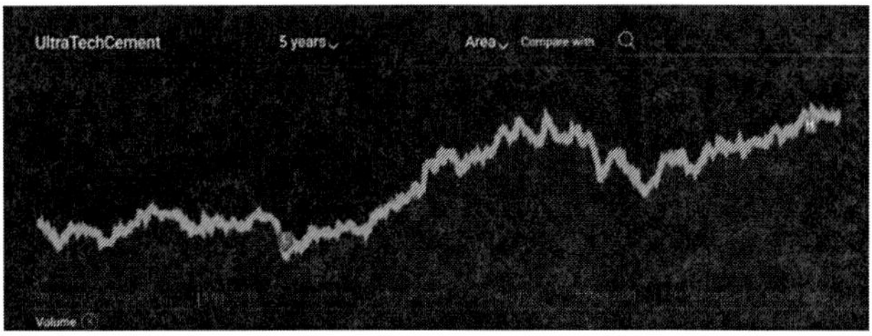

As seen from the above graph, there has been a phenomenal growth of UltraTech Cement in the

last 5 years. The share price of the said stock has risen manifold, from around rs 3000/ in september 2018 to more than rs 8000 in september 2023. If an investor had stayed invested their wealth would also have increased by double which far outweighs investment returns in other instruments like FDs and Mutual funds.

4. Following MEGATREND

Another method of selecting stocks could be by following mega-trend. With new technological advancements new mega-trends is seen emerging every other year. One such example could be the global need to reduce pollution, the introduction of electric vehicles (EV) which are supposed to reduce pollution by several notches. Companies who are manufacturing EVs could be the front runner in this mega-trend. examples of such are Tata motors, Mahindra and Mahindra.

Mega-trends are characterized by being far-reaching global patterns related to behaviour, mobility, and environment. Examples of mega-trends are health, population growth, urbanisation and digitalisation.

Unpredictable markets and changing economic conditions make it hard to know how to know how to invest for the future. Mega-trends offer the potential for enduring growth that transcends interest rate cycles, inflation trends and market volatility.

By focusing on companies that are at the forefront of these transformative trends, investors can position themselves to benefit from the sustained growth and expansion opportunities that mega-trends provide. Firstly, mega-trend investing enables portfolio diversification across various industries and sectors.

Following are the major mega-trends in the present day scenario:

A. SUSTAINABILITY : Sustainability means the development that meets the needs of the present, without compromising the ability of the future generations to meet their own needs.

For too long, economic growth and development has come at an environmental and social cost. With global warming, habitat destruction, poverty and many other socio-economic issues becoming more pressing, it is clear that we need to invest in more sustainable development practices.

Examples of Sustainable Development are :-

1. Wind Energy - Wind turbines are a great solution for power generation due to their cost and the fact that they require a very small land footprint. Conservation and recreation can happen simultaneously with wind power generation.

Top wind power generating industries in India are :

1, TATA Power

2. JSW Energy

3. Torrent power

4. Suzlon Energy

2. Solar Energy -From roof-top solar panels to massive solar farms that can attain same

generational capacity as a conventional power plant, solar energy can bring about a revolution in renewable energy. It can save the earth from so much carbon -dioxide emission. With solar still making up less than 2% of the global energy mix, this shows great potential for the growth of solar in the future.

Best solar energy stocks in India for investment are :

1. Suzlon Energy Limited

2. Tata Power Company

3. Urja Global Limited

4. Adani Green Energy

5. WAA Solar Limited

3. Crop Rotation : Crop rotation is one of the most important practices within sustainable agriculture. It involves planting different crops in the same area at different times of the year or in different years. This method reduces pesticide and herbicide use which can bioaccumulate in species, especially predatory birds. Crop rotation also helps in restoring the soil and increasing its water storing capacity. It has been known to increase the yield of the crops.

This helps agriculture based industries.

Best agriculture Stocks in India are:

1. UPL Ltd.
2. Pi Industries Ltd.
3. Coromandel International Ltd.
4. Bayer Crop Science Ltd.
5. Chambal Fertilizers Ltd.

4. Efficient Water Fixtures : Efficient Water Conserving fixtures and water harvesting are two ways to save water, energy and help sustain the environment.

   Fixtures that save water include low-flow shower heads, sinks with auto-shut off mechanisms. and water saving toilets and urinals. Equipments that save water includes dishwashers, clothes washers and other commercial kitchen equipment such as sprays and steam cookers.

   Some of the companies related to this are:

   1. Hindware
   2. Jaquar
   3. Cera

   In the past investors building their portfolio were often constrained by a home country bias. This geographic approach bled investors to focus on their home markets that they were familiar with, which often caused them to miss some of the best performing global businesses in the past 10 years.

Learning from the success of existing tech-enabledcompanies, three mega-trends have been identified -intelligent machines, genetic science & biotech and 5 G - poised to benefit from the next generation of technology. Mega-trends not only have an economic impact on a global scale but also transform the way we live.

B. Technology in Medicine : One mega-trend has revolutionised available treatments for various life threatening conditions. Robot -assisted surgery (RAS) allows surgeon to use specialised robotic system to perform minimally invasive surgery. Patients can return to work and activity within 10 days of surgery with low risk of complications and infections.

The technology behind intelligent machines, next generation connectivity, and genetic science, positions companies in these Mega-trends to be successful globally

Leading BIOtech companies in India are :

1. Syngene International
2. Biocon
3. GSK Pharma
4. Concord Biotech

Key takeaways from this is

1. Investors need to focus on best performing global businesses following mega-trends
2. Technology change is increasingly driving growth of businesses.
3. Successful companies will need to find ways to scale transformational trends or 'Mega-trends', changing the way we live and work.

POINTS TO KEEP IN MIND WHEN SELECTING STOCKS TO INVEST IN

Once you select a stock to invest following the above given guidelines, there are certain steps that one can follow before actually investing in it. these are : -

1. Keep the stock that you want to invest on your Radar which means keep a track of the company for a week or a month on an App like 'Money Control' or 'Stock Edge'.

2. Check the company. s 52 week high and low, so as not to invest when the share is at its highest. Timing the market is also very important.

3. Check the shareholding i. e how much percentage of shares does the Promoter have and how much does outsiders have. Outsiders can be public or Foreign institutional investors. If promoter has 40% or more shares in the company it means that he has confidence in its own company and is a good sign.

Following is the pie chart of TATA MOTORS

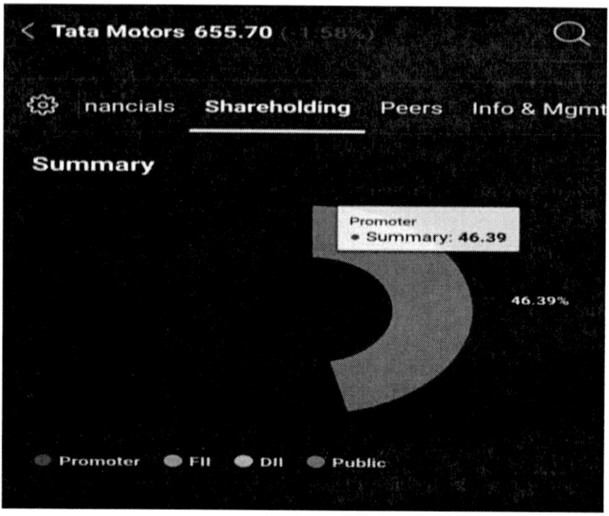

It is clearly showing Promoter's share in shareholding as 46. 39%.

4. Next we can check the graph of the company one wishes to purchase the stock of as to see how the stock has been rising or falling.

   Graph of 'Tata Motors'

   If we see the graph of Tata Motors it has seen consistent rise in the past one month. It was around rs 640/ on 20 th september, went down to a low of rs 608/ on 4 th october, 23, and again started rising reaching its 52 week highest on 16 th October at rs 677/. The rise in the share price has been consistent with the rise in the Automobile sector in India. With the advent of

EV (Electronic Vehicles), in keeping with the rising awareness about sustainability, it is expected to rise further.

5. Another thing we can check about a share one wants to buy is if there has been any big recent deals in the market of the same, like if there has been a bulk buying of the shares

   By a big Bull or by any mutual fund.

6. One should also be updated on any news related to the company whose stock one is about to buy. News can be of any merger or acquisition or splitting of stock or if the company is about to declare dividend. Such happenings can affect the price of the share and one can take an informed decision based on that.

HOW TO MAKE A PORTFOLIO

Suppose one decides to invest a lump sum on shares then how to make a portfolio, so that one has the safety of investment as well as some liquidity to play in the market when the share market rises or falls.

So now that one has decided which company's shares we have to buy based on the various tools discussed earlier, we have to decide how much percentage we should invest in each.

So our main portfolio should be of stocks of highly quality companies which have given consistent returns over the years. Example : Reliance or Hindustan Unilever etc.

Advantage of such companies are that -

1. They provide Capital Protection. Meaning that the amount invested remains safe and does not get eroded. suppose you invested rs 100, 000/ in reliance shares, so this amount will not go down even in worst downfalls. During the outbreak of covid all the shares went drastically down and even Reliance went down, but when the share market started rising it was the first

share to go up. The stock is on the upward journey ever since then and its value is rs 2437/ on september 18th 2023.

2. They are less volatile -which means that their tendency to rise and fall with every news in the market is much less'

3. They require less monitoring : This means that since they are less volatile one need not monitor them on a daily basis as to what is going on in the company, so the time is saved.

But such companies are generally large caps and are quite expensive.

So our main portfolio i. e around 80% of it should be of large scale companies and 20% should be of consistent small caps which can be sold off as and when the market rises or falls. When there is a need for liquidity and the market is expected to rise/fall the shares of these companies can be sold off.

CORPORATE ACTIONS

Corporate actions can significantly impact a company's prospects and share price, so shareholders and investors should keep tabs on them. these events typically need approval by the board of directors and may even require a thumbs up from shareholders.

Corporate actions can be voluntary or mandatory and good or bad. In most cases, activities such as dividend payments, buybacks, and anything else seeking to boost shareholders value are welcome unless investors feel the company's assets could have been used better. Less welcome are Rights issues and liquidation.

So the corporate actions that impact the share price are :

1. Declaration of Dividends
2. Bonus issue
4. Stock split
5. Rights Issue
6. Buyback of shares

1. DIVIDENDS

Dividends are what a company pays to its shareholders out of its profits and reserves as

A form of regular income. Typically, it is paid on a per share basis or as a percentage of

The face value of the share.

Best Indian stocks for long term dividends are :

1. Vedanta

2. Hindustan Zinc

3. Coal India

4. ONGC

5. Power Grid Corporation

6. HCL Technologies

7. REC Ltd.

8. ITC Ltd.

ITC Ltd. has declared dividend two times of rs 12. 25/ in the financial year 2022-2023.

Dividends affect the stock price in several ways. In the short term, share prices often drop when dividend is distributed.

Dividends are generally paid in cash to the shareholders accounts.

Those who sell before the ex-dividend date will not receive any dividend payments. If an investor decides to sell after the ex-dividend date, they will receive whatever the current dividend payment is but will not receive any future payments unless they buy the shares again.

How Some investors track ex-Dividend Dates to capture profits

Dividends capture is essentially a strategy some investors use :

They buy a stock before ex- dividend date and sell it either on a right after the ex-dividend date to capture the dividend

The idea is to "capture" the dividend and sell it on or after the ex-dividend date, either at no loss or no gain, with the dividend kept as profit.

On 29 th may ITC share price rose to a high of rs 451. 8/ and after declaration of dividend on may 30 th it came marginally down and closed at around rs 443/ on june 2nd.

2. BONUS ISSUE

Bonus shares are additional shares issued to the shareholders by the company. For instance, a 1:1 bonus issue means for every share you hold, you get an additional share in the company.

After the bonus issue, the total share value does not decrease or increase as the value per share gets adjusted proportionately.

Example : If one has 100 shares of rs 10 each then after a 1:1 bonus issue, one's holdings become 200 shares of rs 5 / each. The total share value of rs 1000/ does not change, but there is a decline in the value per share, making it easier for small investors to invest.

Recently Power grid corporation of India ltd. announced bonus issue of 1:3 on 08/11/2023, which means for every 3 shares held by the shareholder in the said company he gets 1 share. So if someone holds 30 shares of Power grid, he gets 10 shares as Bonus making his total number of shares as 40.

Most Bonus giving shares in India are :

1. BPCL i. e Bharat Petroleum Corporation ltd.
2. WIPRO
3. INFOSYS
4. ITC
5. GAIL (India)
6. Dabur India

Some of the benefits of the issuance of bonus shares are :

1. Shareholders gain trust in the company after receiving bonus issue It signifies advantage for long term investors.
2. Investors do not need to pay tax on receiving bonus issue.
3. These shares are offered free of cost by the company.
4. The company increases its shareholding and spikes market value with bonus shares.

Disadvantages of Bonus Shares are

1. The company does not receive any cash while issuing bonus shares. As a result, the ability to raise money by following an offering is minimised.
2. When a company keeps on issuing bonus shares instead of dividends, the cost of bonus issued keeps adding up over the years.

Recent example of Bonus issue is Berger Paints

The board of directors of Berger Paints Ltd. declared issuance of bonus shares in 1:5 ratio, which means one bonus share for every five shares held by eligible shareholders of the company, the company board later on declared 23 rd september as record date for issuance of bonus shares on ex-date basis.

Berger paints share witnessed buying interest during early morning deals on 22nd sept. as the stock was trading ex-bonus. After price adjustment, Berger Paints shares opened lower at rs 627. 30/ per share but it soon gained momentum and hit intraday high of 643. 50 per share levels, logging over 2 per cent intraday rise during Friday session.

3. STOCK SPLIT

As the name suggests, a stock split splits the stock into two or more portions. They work on the same principle as Bonus issues. The number of shares with the shareholders increases after a stock split, but the investment value remains the same.

Suppose a company declares a 1:2 stock split. The face value of stock you hold is rs 10/. If before the split you held 25 shares, after split, you will hold 50 shares. The face value will change to rs 5 per share, keeping the total investment value of rs 250 / intact.

Generally, stock splits happen when a company's share prices are quiet high, and the company wants to bring them down to encourage more investors, it increases liquidity in the company.

Recent example of Stock Split is Tata Steel

One of the top global steel companies, Tata Steel split its stock in the ratio 1:10 in june 2022. It means that every shareholder got 10 shares for every single holding. The share started quoting on an ex-split basis from July 28, 2022. If someone had 20 shares of Tata steel then after the split it becomes 200 shares, but the value remains the same.

The value of Tata Steel share went down by 1/10 th after the Stock split. For example if The tata steel stock was trading near rs 1000/ before the stock split after that it came down to rs 100/. Meanwhile, the stock hit an intra day high of rs 109. 30, later it closed at rs 107. 80, rising 7. 42% on BSE. , after the split.

On 25 th september Tata Steel was trading at rs 127. 40 / and is expected to rise further.

4. RIGHTS ISSUE

A rights issue is when a company issues additional shares to its existing shareholders instead of the public at large. unlike bonus shares, you need to actually pay money to buy these shares, usually at a discounted price. For example, a 1:5 rights issue means for every 5 shares you hold, you can subscribe to 1 additional share.

A company may go in for a rights issue to finance its expansion or debt reduction. Hence, it is important that one subscribe to these shares only if one is confident about the company's future.

Let us take an example where Reena, an existing shareholder of company ABC, owns 20 shares of rs 200 each. The company issues right of shares to Reena and offers a discount of 30% and allows her one share for every two existing shares. As a result Reena can buy ten right-issue shares of rs 140 each.

- Investor's portfolio value before rights issue = 20 shares into rs 200 =rs 4000
- Number of right shares to be received = 20 *1/2 =10
- Price to be paid to buy rights issue = 10 shares * rs 140=rs 1400
- Total number of shares after rights issue = 20 + 10 = 30
- Revised value of the portfolio after exercising rights issue = rs 4000 + rs 1400=rs 5400/
- Price per share post rights issue = rs 5400/30 =rs 180/

Theoretically the price of the share after right issue should be rs 180/, but that is not how the market behaves. An uptrend in the share price will benefit the investor, while if the price falls below rs 180 /, the investor will lose money.

Key Takeaways :

- The rights issue is basically a way through which a listed company raises additional funds.
- An investor should be able to look beyond the discount offered. He is paying money to get additional shares, so he should subscribe to it

only if he is completely sure of the company's performance and future potential.

- EPS, book value per share metrics decline because of the higher number of shares.
- If the promoter is taking part in the Rights issue of shares then it can be a positive sign.

5. BUYBACK OF SHARES

A buyback of shares is when a company buys its shares from the shareholders to consolidate its stake in the enterprise. Usually, the shares are bought at a premium to reduce the number of outstanding shares in the market. This increases earnings per share. A buyback is seen in a positive light as a sign reflecting the company's confidence in itself. Some other reasons for buyback include :

- Preventing other companies from taking over
- Preventing the share price from going too low
- Building investors confidence in the promoters

Example :

L & T announced buyback of shares on 26 th july. It is first such offer in its eight - decade long history. It offered to buy back a 2. 4% stake, or 33. 33 million shares, held by public shareholders through a book-building process on the stock exchange. The eligible shareholders can tender their shares for a buyback price of rs 3, 200/ per share. The last date for tendering shares is September 25, 2023. The buyback is at a premium of around 10. 5% to the closing price on September 20.

After the Buy- back L&T has seen consistent rise in price, on 29th it was trading at rs 3031/per share.

Based on forecasts "L&T"stock price is expected to rise to around rs 5000/ in another 5 years.

Thus while the number of shares in circulation falls, shareholders ' stake in the company and the amount they are due from future dividends increases, as a result of Buy-back.

Important Takeaways

Corporate actions can significantly impact a company's prospects and share price. Thus it is important to understand and keep tabs on them. What happens when bonus shares are issued to evaluate a company's worth. A rights issue may drive the share prices down with an increase in the number of shares in the market.

Whereas a buyback may create a sudden temporary spike in the share prices as there is a reduction in the availability of the outstanding shares in the market.

Understanding these corporate actions can help you decide whether you wish to buy or sell your shares.

INITIAL PUBLIC OFFER (IPO)

An initial public offering (IPO) refers to the process of offering shares of a private corporation to the public in a new stock issuance for the first time. An IPO allows a company to raise equity capital from public investors. It could be a new, young company or an old company which decides to be listed on an exchange and hence goes public. An IPO is typically underwritten by one or more investment banks, who also arrange for the shares to be listed on one or more stock exchanges.

By investing in an IPO, one can enter at the starting point of the company i.e at a 'low level 'of a company with a high growth potential. An IPO could be your window to rapid profit in a short time period. It may also help you grow your wealth in the long run.

There is a growing trend among investors to invest in any IPO to take advantage of the listing gains. But after the debacle of PAYTM IPO one should understand that even the most hyped and over subscribed IPO can fail the investors.

The PAYTM IPO was the country's biggest IPO and was subscribed 1. 89 times with institutional buyers including FII s flooding the share sale. On the day of listing the stock closed over 27% lower at rs 1564/ per share from the issue price.

An informed investor should assess an IPO on several factors before investing their hard earned money.

FACTORS to keep in mind before applying for an IPO are :

1. Company's Financials

Before investing in an IPO, one should know about the company's financials as much as possible. This means company's performance in last few years, the profit made by the company, revenue generated etc. One should subscribe to an IPO only if that company is financially sound.

All this information can be found in the Draft Red Herring Prospectus (DRHP), it is a document that a company needs to file with Securities and Exchange Board of India (SEBI), to get approval for issuing an IPO. One can also visit the company's website.

2. Promoters of the Company

An important thing to look for when subscribing to an IPO is the Company's promoters and management team.

Companies with strong and experienced promoters usually have strong. growth potential. The shares of such companies usually appreciate considerably over the time

And give good returns to the shareholders.

3. Company's Strengths and Risks

Every company has its own strengths and risks. Conducting a SWOT (Strengths, Weaknesses, Opportunities and Threats) analysis of a company before investing in its IPO is crucial. If the strengths outweigh the risk then one can place the bid.

For example if a company has good market share and has an efficient distribution network to cater to its customers. its IPO can provide good returns.

All issuing companies mention their strengths and risks in the DRHP's. One can also visit the Motilal Oswal website to know about strengths and weaknesses of a company whenever a new IPO is announced.

4. The Valuation of the IPO

The valuation of an IPO depends on the price at which shares are issued to the investors the first time. It is one of the most crucial factors to be analyzed before subscribing to an IPO. One should not subscribe to an IPO if it seems overvalued.

Like it happened in the case of' PAYTM ' IPO (It was valued at a high of rs 2150, got listed at rs

1950/and went into relentless decline closing at rs 944. 50/ in 3 months).

However if an IPO looks fairly valued one can bid for it to get good returns.

The best way to decide if an IPO is fairly valued is by comparing the issue price with the prices of shares belonging to similar companies.

5. Prevailing market conditions

Last but not the least, one must look at the current market conditions before subscribing to an IPO. If the markets are bullish, at the time of IPO then it is most likely to be open in green. However, even the best IPOs tend to open in red or offer less returns during the bearish market.

Prevailing market conditions carry more significance if you invest in an IPO only for listing gains. However if one plans to hold shares long - term, in that case one should emphasise on looking at company's fundamentals, IPO valuation and other factors mentioned before.

CASE STUDY OF RR KABEL IPO

Let us consider the case study of RR Kabel IPO. RR Kabel produces consumer electrical products that are used for comprehensive purposes such as residential, industrial, commercial, and infrastructure purposes. The company operates in two main segments 1. Wires and 2. Cables. RR Kabel caters to diverse clientele, spanning both domestic and international markets. The IPO was listed on 26 th September 2023 on the stock exchanges. The price band per share was rs 983/ to rs 1035/ and the lot size was 14 shares

Axis capital Ltd., HSBC Securities and Capital Markets(India) Private Ltd., Citigroup Global Markets India Private Ltd. , and JM Financial Ltd. are the book running lead managers for this IPO, while Link Intime India Private Ltd, is the registrar.

Objectives of R. R. KABEL IPO :

1. Prepay or repay full/part of the debt obtained from the banks and financial institutions.

2. Funds for general corporate purposes.

Peer Comparison

- Havells India Ltd.
- KEI Industries Ltd.
- Polycab India Ltd.
- Finolex Cables Ltd.

As we can understand after studying the above companies and their share prices which ranges from rs 950/ to rs 5000/ of Polycab Cables, the price of RR Kabel seems rightly valued.

Strengths of RR Kabel

- The company has over 20 years of track record and a scaled B2C business in the large and growing wires and cables business'
- PAN-India and global presence.

It is the fastest -growing consumer electrical company amongst its peers in India, growing at a CAGR of 43. 4% between FY 2021 and FY 2023 *

Technologically advanced and integrated precision manufacturing facilities.

- It is well- positioned for growth in the FMEG segment.
- Experienced management team.

Risks

- Negative cash flows in the past.
- Higher working-capital requirements.
- Volatility in raw material prices can impact the company's operations.
- The overseas market is dependent on a few distributors and any changes in business arrangements with these distributors may impact RR Kabel 's financials.
- Prone to forex market fluctuations.
- Unsecured loans from banks and other financial institutions, which may be recalled on demand.

As seen from the above SWOT analysys that although there are number of weaknesses

But it has very strong strengths which can overcome the weaknesses after some time.

As expected RR Kabel debuted on NSE on 20 th september at rs 1, 180/ a premium of 14% over IPO price of rs 1, 035 per share. In around one month it already rose to around rs 1500/. It is still expected to rise further giving stelling returns to its shareholders.

MERGER AND ACQUISITION(M & A)

A merger is a process in which two or more companies unite to form a single entity. It results in a creation of a new company, which often takes the names of all the companies involved in the merger (example. Metro Goldwyn -Mayer Studios was formed by combining Metro pictures, Goldwyn Pictures, and Louis B, Mayer Pictures).

Mergers are usually friendly and intricately planned, and there is no power difference between merged entities.

M & A revolves around a company's growth strategy. The M&A take place in the

Company in order to increase market share, geographical outreach, reduce competition, earn profits from patents or even enter into new sectors or product lines.

One of the major reasons for the increasing mergers is the increasing competition. The effects of increased competition are more evident in companies from the e-commerce industry. This industry has paved way for some of the most aggressive M&A in the recent past

Some of the Recent Mergers in India has been :

1. Zee Entertainment and Sony India merger.
2. Indus towers - Bharti Airtel merger.
3. Tata Group / Air India
4. PVR/INOX Merger
5. HDFC LTD/HDFC BANK Merger

India's largest housing finance company HDFC Ltd. and the largest private bank. HDFC Bank, merged in 2022 in one of the biggest financial deals in India. The $40 billion deal will result in a single entity, but the services of HDFC Ltd. and HDFC Bank will continue to be provided separately.

The last few years have been financially volatile for not just everyday folks but even billion dollar corporations as well.

In 2022, several high profile acquisitions and mergers took place. Some happened due to personal vendettas, some to bail out a failing company, but most mergers and acquisitions transpired to increase profits.

KEY TAKEAWAYS OF A&M are

- When one company acquires another, stock price of acquiring company tends to dip temporarily, while the stock price of target company tends to spike.

- The aquiring company's share price drops because it often pays a premium for the target company, or incurs debt to finance the acquisition.
- The target company;s short-term share price tends to rise because the shareholders only agree to the deal if the purchase price exceeds their company;s current value.
- Over the long haul, an acquisition tends to boost the acquiring company;s share price.

DE –MERGER

A demerger is when a company splits off one or more divisions to operate independently or to be sold off. A demerger may take place for several reasons such as -

*Focusing on a company's core operations

* Spinning off less relevant business units

* To raise Capital

* To discourage a hostile takeover

The new company may not necessary be a subsidiary of a parent company after the split.

A demerger is a corporate partition of a company into smaller undertakings, where one separated undertaking is retained by a parent company while others are either acquired by other, work independently, liquidated, or are sold.

Recently Reliance industries demerged its financial services into Reliance Strategic Investments as part of its group restructuring. The spun off entity has been renamed Jio Financial Services Ltd. (JFSL). It had sought approval of shareholders in May, for this to create value to shareholders.

The ratio for demerger was set at 1:1. For each share held in Reliance Industries as on record date (i. e July 20), one share of JFSL was credited. That means shareholders who had bought Reliance Industries shares on or before July 19, received JFSL shares.

Experts said that the demerger decision was taken to keep the financial business distinct from other businesses to attract a different set of investors, strategic partners. lenders and other shareholders. Post demerger, aim is to lend consumers and merchants based on propriety data analytics and eventually branch out into insurance, payments, digital broking and asset management.

HOW WAS THE PRICE OF JIO FINANCIAL SERVICES DISCOVERED

On July 20 th 2023 after the end of a special pre-open auction session on stock exchanges, the market price of Jio Financial Services(JFSL) was derived at rs 261. 85 / per share on NSE, much higher than brokerage estimates of up to rs 190/.

Taking into account the impact of the demerger, the share price of Reliance Industries (RIL) fell to rs 2, 580/ but rallied up to 2% after normal trading resumed after 10 am.

HOW TO SELECT WINNING STOCKS

Earlier we have covered how to select good quality stocks and make a portfolio. We have discussed that 80% of the portfolio value should be invested in large caps which give consistent returns and capital protection and rest 20% should be in consistent and good small caps or mid caps. But small or mid caps can become large caps and give multibagger returns. There are certain rules to identifying winning stocks which are on the verge of becoming multibagger 'These can be as follows:

RULE 1

The winning stocks are like eagle trading near 85% value of 52 week high and continuously making higher highs and showing strong earning growth.

The all-time high stocks breakout after a gap of 15 to 24 months give us a big indication of a winner.

Example : If we take Reliance industries example, it was in a decade long consolidation after the great financial crisis of 2007, in mid 2017 it was around rs 500/. But ever since 2017, the stock started rising and rose to a staggering five times within a short span of 5 years. It was quoting at a price of rs 2, 825/ in July 2023.

Rule 2

THE PRICING POWER OF BRANDING

In the history of capital markets all multibaggers have focussed on strong brand creation thereby reinforcing there position in the marketplace, attracting better quality customers with higher retention rates and raising the perceived value of their products or services. Examples of such strong brands in India are :

1. MARUTI
2. ITC
3. RELIANCE
4. EICHER MOTORS
5. HINDUSTAN UNILEVER
6. TATA MOTORS

Key to understanding winners

*To look and understand their product pipeline

* New launch in the existing market

* New launch in a different market

* Creating a brand new market

* Fulfilment of the needs of their customers

RULE 3:

INVEST IN BUSINESS NOT THE PRICE

The winners generally have successful business models and are more expensive.

An amount of rs 1000/ invested in Reliance is more than Rupees 16, 00, 000 in 40 years

An amount of rs 1000/ invested in Eicher Motors is more than Rupees 1, 00, 000 in 8 years

Winning stocks provide strong CAGR (Compound annual growth rate) over a period of time

Points to remember are :

- Investors should not make a mistake of looking at a shorter time frame only.
- One should never make a mistake of finding undervalued or over- valued companies by looking at their prices.
- Winning stocks will always look expensive in relative comparison to markets.

The most expensive share in the Indian stock exchange is MRF, or MadrasRubberFactory Ltd. was at rs 6595/ in 2010 and has now risen to an astounding price of rs 1, 10, 000 in october 2023.

RULE 4 :

WHO HOLDS THE MOST

As we have done earlier in how to select the stocks, The equity capital holders consist of 3 major categories

- PROMOTERS
- INSTITUTIONAL INVESTORS
- OTHERS Category

The key here is to track the fund flow of promoters, institutional and big investors if they are investing into their company by increasing or decreasing their stake.

Promoters and institutional investors are informed investors and they understand the business structure of any company from a fundamental perspective.

Higher demand leads to higher prices thereby reducing the supply (floating stock) and similarly lower demand leads to higher supply.

The shareholding pattern report is published quarterly by every listed company which gives details of shareholding pattern.

RULE 5

WINNERS SURVIVE

Bull markets on an average lasts for more than two years which is a good time for an investor to generate a big return and one should understand these macro points to catch the bulls market because identifying in the early stages can help him to hold on to winners.

The common features of a BULL MARKET are :

*Stable government at the centre

* Lower or stable crude prices

* Strong FII and DII flows into equity and debt markets

* Strong or lower interest rates thereby spurring corporate growth

* Stable earning growth

RULE 6 :

INVESTING IN STOCKS THAT HAVE VALUE BUT AT MAXIMUM PESSIMISM

- There is a saying in financial markets that "Trouble is an opportunity ". There are certain Macro and Micro events which pulls the market valuations down. Example like how market crashed when Covid broke out and then again recovered after more than a year. The top resilient stocks were : Reliance Industries, SBI, Larsen & Toubro, Bajaj Finserv, Titan Ind, , Sun Pharma, ONGC and Tata Steel.

One should always look to buy these winning stocks at point of maximum pessimism as Warren Buffet did when he bought Goldman Sachs in 2008 crises as Behavioural Finance states in period of irrational turbulence there lies value.

RULE 7 :

CASH IS THE KEY

Cash flow is the net amount of cash and cash equivalents moving in and out of the business Cash flow is divided into three parts :

* Cash flow from operating activities

* Cash flow from investing activities

* Cash flow from financing activities

- Every winning company will be increasing cash flow from operating activities on a year on year basis as the cash generated from business will be used for expansion and developing new products thereby giving it the margin of safety.

RULE 8

SECTOR ROTATION IS THE KEY

- Winning stocks generally belong to a sector or a group and in bull market over the one year time frame the individual stock/sector outperforms the benchmark indices, but due to short term market noise it is available at a correction in the one week to one month time frame with lower volumes.

- These stocks can be bought when the prices move upward supported by volumes spurt

And delivery percentage.

Graph of Nifty Auto of last 5 years

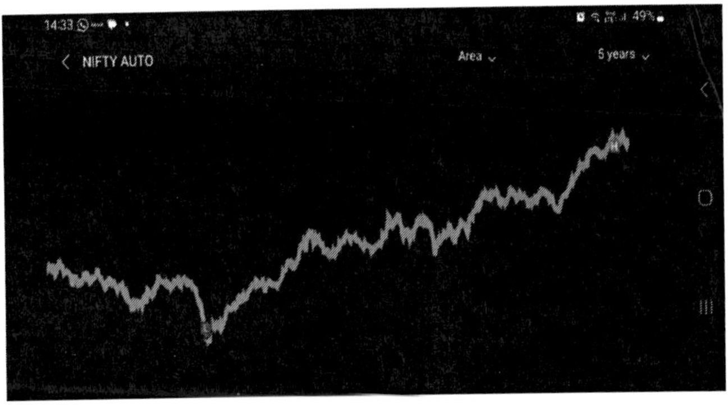

As we can see from the above graph, the Auto sector has been doing very well in the last 5 years. It came down in march 2020 at the onset of covid to around rs 4000/, only to consistently rise ever since and has recently made a high of around rs 16, 000/.

If we see the graph of TATA MOTORS which is a part of Nifty Auto, it has mirrored the consistent growth of its sector. From rs 70 in march 2020 to above rs 600/ in september 2023. Its growth has been even more than its sector.

STRATEGY FOR SECTOR ROTATION ENTRY FOR STOCKS

- In a one year time frame the stock as well as benchmark index should be giving positive returns.
- In the three months time frame the stock should outperform the benchmark index by minimum 5 %(large cap), 10 % for midcap and small cap.
- Once these two conditions are met we should look for those areas where the markets have given small price based corrections from recent high and try to enter on the breakout of recent high and confirm with high volume and delivery percentage.

Rule 9

IDENTIFYING POTENTIAL LEADERS

- Leaders of today may not be leaders of tomorrow. Evolution and adaptation is the key to survival even in the stock market. Only one company, General Electric is in the original Dow 30 component, rest 29 companies have moved out of Dow 30 stock index list.

- As time changes so do the opportunities and challenges, companies which do not adapt and evolve will move out of the winners list.
- The investor of winning stocks understands the market trends and only book profits when they understand that the business dynamics have changed and the current model is no longer relevant.
- Markets are always correct and when market prices start to show underperformance over long term periods then investors should evaluate their exit decision on other market facts.
- As investors one has to anticipate future trend changes and must understand the company's vision for the coming years.
- One good Tip is to follow big investors who hold more than 1% stake in the company. Investors like : Rakesh Jhunjhunwala, Radhakrishna Damani, Dolly Khanna, Porinju Veliyath, Ashish Kacholia etc. These investors track the companies and have big stakes in companies they invest in. They invest with proper research and continuously track their investment.

RULE 10

MONEY MANAGEMENT IS THE KEY TO PROSPERITY

- Research has shown that only 10% of socks listed in the markets outperform in the markets. The key is to build the portfolio of those stocks and hold them until they grow manifold.
- Money management rules include
- The amount of allocation of individual stocks in the portfolio with related diversification in various market sectors.
- Proper entry and exit rules. The entry and exit rules should be clear and devoid of all emotions.

SOME EXCELLENT QUOTES BY VARIOUS GURUS OF SHARE MARKET ARE

BY WARREN BUFFET

- Never depend on one single income. Make investment to create a second source
- If you buy things you don't need soon you will be selling things you need.
- Do not save what is left after spending, but spend what is left after saving '

By RAKESH JHUNJHUNWALA

- Always go against tide, Buy when others are selling and sell when others are buying
- Prepare for losses 'Losses are part and parcel of stock market investor life

KEEP IT SIMPLE

Last but not the least, listen to your GUT. Keep your research simple, big money is made by holding conviction to your investment ideas.

By keeping research simple one should develop clear entry and exit so that one is not guided by market forces. One should sometimes book profits and sometimes cut the losses.

One is constantly learning in the market, one should have one's one evaluation of performance of the stocks held so that one grows and evolve as an investor.